REAL Reflections

Inspiring Quotes for Empowered Living

Dr. Teri Rouse
Educator, Early & Behavior Interventionist, Autism & Reading Specialist

R*E*A*L* Reflections
Inspiring Quotes for Empowered Living

drterirouse.com

Copyright © 2024 Dr. Teri Rouse

All rights reserved

No portion of this book may be reproduced mechanically, electronically, or by any other means, including photocopying, without securing the advanced written permission of the author. Likewise, no portion of this book may be posted to a website or distributed by any other means without securing the advanced written permission of the author.

Limits of liability and disclaimer of warranty

This book is strictly for informational and educational purposes only. The author and the publisher shall not be liable for any misuse of the enclosed material. The author and the publisher do not guarantee that any one following these techniques, suggestions, tips, ideas, or strategies will be successful or healed. The author and the publisher shall have neither liability nor responsibility to anyone with respect to any loss or damage caused, or alleged to be caused, directly or indirectly, by the information or suggestions contained in this book.

Published by Made to Change the World™ Publishing
Nashville, Tennessee

Cover and interior design by Chelsea Jewell

ISBN: 978-1-956837-37-7 Hardback

Printed in the USA, Canada, Australia, and Europe

To those of you who want to discover your resilient self and unlock your inner power so that you can transform fear into autonomy and create your extraordinary life. May your journey through these pages, through the words of wise people, inspire you to trust the strength within and embrace the limitless possibilities ahead.

CONTENTS

Foreword — vii

Acknowledgments — ix

Introduction — xiii

Chapter 1 — 1

R*E*A*L*

Overview of R*E*A*L* — 1
R = Resilience — 3
E = Empowerment — 4
A = Autonomy — 6
L = Extraordinary Living — 6

Chapter 2 — 9

Resilience: Bouncing Back Stronger

From Spark to Fire — 9
Embracing Vulnerability as Strength — 11
Practicing Resilience Daily — 50

Chapter 3 — 53

Empowerment: Transforming from Within

The True Meaning of Personal Power — 53
Finding Your Voice — 55
Empowerment Through Action: Persistence and Determination — 94

Chapter 4   97
Autonomy in Action

> The Power of Making Your Own Choices   97
> Embracing Your Personal Freedom   100
> Celebrating Your Autonomy: Living a Life True
> to Yourself   140

Chapter 5   143
Step Into Extraordinary Living

> Embracing Your Unique Journey   143
> What Is Extraordinary Living?   145

Chapter 6   185
Looking Back With Gratitude, Moving Forward With Hope

> A Life Well-Lived: Celebrating Your Achievements
> and Milestones   187

A Note from Me to You   189

About the Author   191

Foreword

As I reflect on the journey that my incredible wife, Dr. Teri Rouse, has taken, I am filled with a deep sense of admiration and pride. When she first told me about her vision for *R*E*A*L* Reflections: Inspiring Quotes for Empowered Living*, I knew it would be something extraordinary, just like everything she pours her heart and soul into. This book is more than a compilation of inspiring words; it is a testament to her unwavering resilience, boundless compassion, and profound wisdom.

Teri's journey has not been an easy one. She has faced adversity with grace, transformed challenges into opportunities, and emerged from each trial stronger and more determined. Her experiences have shaped her into a beacon of hope and empowerment, not just for herself, but for everyone fortunate enough to cross her path. I have witnessed firsthand how her commitment to helping others has created ripples of positive change in countless lives.

In this book, Teri shares her personal reflections and the quotes that have inspired her along her journey. Each quote is carefully chosen, resonating with her own experiences and the lessons she has learned. Through these words, she offers readers a chance to tap into their own strength, to find solace in times of struggle, and to discover the courage to create a life that is not just lived, but cherished.

What makes this book truly special is the personal touch that Teri brings to every page. Her stories are raw and authentic, a reflection of the person she is—resilient, empowering, and ever so genuine. She has an incredible gift for connecting with people, for seeing their potential even when they cannot see it themselves, and for inspiring them to reach for the extraordinary.

I have had the privilege of walking alongside Teri as her partner, confidant, and cheerleader. I have seen her rise from the ashes of past hardships, guided by an unyielding belief in the power of transformation. Her journey has been a testament to the incredible strength of the human spirit and the limitless possibilities that come when we embrace our true selves.

To the readers of this book, I offer my heartfelt encouragement. Allow Teri's words to guide you, to uplift you, and to ignite the spark within you. Embrace the lessons, reflect on your own journey, and let this book be a source of inspiration and empowerment. Remember, just as Teri has found her path to an extraordinary life, so, too, can you. The power lies within you, waiting to be unleashed.

Teri, my love, thank you for being the incredible person you are. Your resilience, empowerment, and dedication to creating an extraordinary life have not only transformed your own world, but have touched the hearts and lives of so many others. I am proud to stand by your side and to witness the positive impact you continue to make.

With all my love and admiration,

Dr. Fred Rouse

Acknowledgments

There are so many people who have influenced my path in life that I cannot name every one. However, I want to acknowledge some of the people and groups who have impacted me in remarkable ways along this journey and without whom this book would not have been possible.

My husband, Dr. Fred: For recognizing my resilience, encouraging me to use my empowered voice, supporting the expansion of my autonomy, and for cocreating this extraordinary life we are living!

My mom and my sister: For your persistent and consistent resilience in managing both the everyday and the extraordinary challenges in life!

My daughter, Kristen: For being my forever valentine and who, from a very young age, modeled strength you did not even know you had.

Dr. Jessica Kahn: For always being on my heels to be the best I can be and encouraging me to step into my greatness.

Sister Marie Bambrick: For being my friend and confidant, my cheerleader, my connection creator, and my dear neighbor.

Francine: First, for being my daughter's teacher; second, for sharing our passion for travel; and, third, for always encouraging me to write and speak my mind through the lens of empowering others to find their own voice.

The members of *Joys and Challenges of Relative Caregivers*: For your honest feedback and consistent support during the writing and publishing process.

Ann Clemens Dixon: For encouraging good conversation around raising grandchildren and encouraging people to ask for help when they need it.

My Sedona Sisters: You will all always be in my heart! I hear you, I see you, I am with you. I am forever grateful for your love and support.

Angel and Suzi: Thank you for your love and support throughout the years! You have been true cheerleaders and friends.

Pontheolla and Paul: For the beauty of your words, the love from your hearts, and the inspiration you have radiated.

My book-writing bootcamp champions: For your words, ideas, input, and critique throughout the writing process. I'm grateful.

Shelley Rannels: My friend throughout chaos and calm, near and far.

Dr. Jonathan Moselle: For talking me off the ledge countless times and reminding me that I am perfectly imperfect.

Jack Canfield and Patty Aubery: For helping me to see my value and purpose and helping me share it with the world.

Lisa Nichols: For your powerful reminder that "You are not alone."

Meredith Breitstein: For years of friendship, encouragement, and teaching me how to let myself shine.

Dr. Jill Biden: For demonstrating strength and grace in the most challenging situations.

Jane Goodall: For all things humane. Thank you for sharing your bright light with our world.

Chelsea, Stephanie, Megan, and Milla: For being my dream team. You have made all things possible through web design, editing, photography, and social media … and friendship.

And last, but certainly *not* least, Ellie: For pushing me out of my comfort zone, helping me refine who I am and what I am meant to do so I can serve who

I am meant to serve, and traveling the world with me (hello, London, hello, France … who knows where next!). But, most importantly, for being my friend. Love you … mean it.

Introduction

For over twenty years, I have worked with children and their families to help improve communication, resolve conflicts, and restore peace in their lives—at home, in school, and as part of their community. I have been a teacher, an instructional assistant, a behavior and early interventionist, a reading and autism specialist, a coach, a consultant, a facilitator, a student, and a mentor.

Every classroom, home, or community center I have entered has left a mark on me. Some of those "marks" were extremely positive; others … not so much. But one thing I learned over all the years of helping other families is that I need creative ways to remain positive and find—and keep—*my* peace.

Even today, with all of my experience, I still need to find ways to build my resilience, lean into my self-empowerment, own my autonomy, and live my own extraordinary life, not just pass my time here on Earth.

There are a lot of really smart people in the world whose words offer powerful insights that we can use for our own good. Sometimes, what needs to be said has already been said. These people inspire me and help me fill my cup when I need it. Lisa Nichols embodies the very essence of resilience, empowerment, autonomy, and extraordinary living. Temple Grandin has influenced the way we work with people who think differently. Walt Disney understood that if you can dream it, you can do it! Carol Burnett, Betty White, and Lucille Ball have made us laugh until we cried! Colin Powell has been a strong and thoughtful influence in our country. And Martin Luther King Jr., Gandhi, and Nelson Mandela have changed the world and the way we live in it. These are just a few of the people whose words have influenced who I am, what I do, and why I do it.

I have chosen some of my favorite quotes from a wide variety of people in the hope that some, a lot, or, possibly, all of their words will resonate with you. My hope is that you will find the motivation and inspiration to unleash your resilience, discover your empowered self, harness your autonomy, and create your extraordinary life!

The book is divided into four sections: Resilience, Empowerment, Autonomy, and Extraordinary Living. Each section has a series of quotes and stories that have inspired, motivated, and prompted me to address my own life's challenges through a different lens. The quotes are the words from people you may, or may not, know. The people in the stories are R*E*A*L*, only their names have been changed to protect their privacy.

Lisa Nichols says, "We can change the way our next chapter will be written because we are still holding the pen in our hands." After each series of stories and quotes, I have provided you with a place to express your thoughts and feelings about what you are reading. Whether you jot down your thoughts, create a list, or simply doodle, this exercise will help you rediscover your spark and ignite your power from within. Do whatever works for you.

I hope that you laugh until you cry. I hope that you find words that bring you peace and words that inspire you to be the best version of yourself. But, most of all, I hope this book helps you think outside the proverbial box and see the beautiful life that you can have and that you deserve!

— Dr. Teri Rouse, Ed.D.

Chapter 1

R*E*A*L*

I want to be free and free indeed and live and live abundant!

— Kathie Lee Gifford

Overview of R*E*A*L*

Before we go any further, I want to talk about R*E*A*L*. Why? Because resilience, empowerment, autonomy, and extraordinary living are the foundation for moving through the muck and into the light. Understanding these ideas is how you find the strength, independence, and peace you crave and satisfy your longing to discover your very special and individual superpowers and your gifts.

These four ideas, when put together, become the foundation for building strong people. Strong people build strong connections. Strong connections create strong communities. And strong communities contribute to creating extraordinary lives!

R*E*A*L REFLECTIONS

Let's face it, there is and always will be chaos. And while it can't be avoided, it can be mastered. When you face challenges with resilience and with the expectation of improving yourself and your life, you use the muscles that grow with every hurdle, every argument, and every negative soundtrack you have ever heard. Now is the time to use these muscles and create the life you want for yourself.

Let me start with a story that rocked my world and made me rethink what I wanted out of life. I couldn't believe it. I was absolutely terrified. I was going to ask for a divorce … NO … I was going to demand a divorce. I was terrified to speak my truth. I was terrified that I wouldn't be able to survive. I was mortified at the thought that I would have to ask for help. BUT … I had to. I had to get away, and I had to take my daughter with me. I knew I had to do it, but still the questions I had asked myself for so many years continued to be the soundtrack I heard over and over again. How was I going to do this? Where was I going to go? How was I going to pay for everything? Where would we live? Was I strong enough to do this? I believe every person attempting to navigate through the chaos and challenges of life will recognize these questions. Chaos doesn't look the same to everyone, but the one question that each person usually asks themselves in the midst of it is: How did I get here?

Have you ever asked yourself any or all of these questions? In your own life, maybe it wasn't a divorce but another situation that had you reeling and seeking answers for the pain.

With resilience I didn't know I possessed, yet empowered to make a decision on my own knowing that I would learn and grow to be independent and autonomous, and understanding that the quality of my and my daughter's lives would only improve once I made the decision, I found my voice. I roused my courage and my commitment, and I walked away. Actually, I ran. I ran away from the comforts of my little house on my little green acre (it was familiar, not comfortable, and I had to learn that they are not the same thing), and I never looked back. There were days where I could rely on my own strength to carry me, and there were days where I could not. On those days, I sought solace in words. Words that made me deep-belly laugh and words that made me let go and cry. Words that allowed me to open my heart and to open my mind. Words that helped me to be honest with myself and see the bigger picture and words that helped me grow into the person I am today. These pages are filled with those words.

Following, you will find quotes from remarkable individuals who have successfully built and shared their own R*E*A*L* with the world. But you don't have to be famous to be resilient; you don't have to be loud to be empowered; you don't have to be alone to be autonomous; and you don't have to be surrounded by fans to have an extraordinary life. All the people in this book put their pants on one leg at a time … just like you. Resilience, empowerment, autonomy, and extraordinary living—R*E*A*L*—are not reserved for the rich and famous. They are attainable by anyone willing to go after them.

Thus, interspersed between the quotes are examples of ordinary people who have demonstrated resilience, empowerment, autonomy, and a commitment to extraordinary living. So what do these qualities actually look like?

Resilience is found in everyday challenges. It's not just about bouncing back from setbacks. It is also about navigating daily struggles with grace and determination. Empowerment can be harnessed through small acts of self-belief. It involves recognizing your own worth and taking control of your life even in the face of adversity. Autonomy is gained by making independent choices that align with your values and reflect your true self. Extraordinary living is finding joy and meaning in the ordinary, delight and purpose in the everyday moments. Through these real-life examples, you will see that these qualities are not impossibilities but practical traits that anyone can develop and incorporate into their lives. By embracing these principles, you, too, can build a R*E*A*L* life filled with purpose and fulfillment, just like the folks in this book.

R = Resilience

Building a Resilient Mindset

Having resilience and being resilient means that you can gather your inner strength in circumstances where strength is difficult to come by. This inner strength helps you respond to the challenges that you face in a way that keeps you calm and in control even when you feel threatened. It also allows you to bounce back from those challenges without being overwhelmed and overcome by them. During my season of leaving my home and preparing for a divorce, I fortified my resilience by using the words of wise people to help me believe that better days were coming and that no matter what my life looked like at the time, I was fighting for something extraordinary.

An exceptional example of resilience is Nelson Mandela, who spent twenty-seven years in prison under South Africa's apartheid reign. What sets Mandela apart is not just the duration of his incarceration, but how he emerged from it with an unwavering commitment to reconciliation and unity. Despite facing immense personal suffering and witnessing the injustices of apartheid firsthand, Mandela chose a path of forgiveness rather than revenge upon his release. This decision was pivotal in averting a potential civil war in South Africa. His ability to rise above bitterness and lead his nation toward reconciliation is a testament to his remarkable resilience. Emotions undoubtedly played a significant role in Mandela's journey; from the initial anger and frustration at his unjust imprisonment to the eventual triumph of forgiveness and peace. His journey reflects the essence of resilience, demonstrating how one can harness emotions to overcome hardships and steer toward a brighter future.

E = Empowerment

Empowerment Through Self-Belief

Empowerment means having control over your thoughts, choices, and your life. It means knowing your options and having the courage to make choices based on what you want. It means discovering the tools and skills needed to become confident and independent in order to navigate life's challenges. First, clear communication, both in expressing thoughts and understanding others, is key. Clear communication empowers you to convey your ideas effectively. Next, problem-solving abilities help you navigate chaos and challenges, empowering you to face adversity with strength. Effective time management ensures you complete tasks efficiently, empowering you to take control of your schedule and priorities. Becoming more self-aware helps you understand your personal strengths and weaknesses. This empowers you to make informed decisions.

CHAPTER 1: R*E*A*L*

Finally, consistently being willing to learn and adapt encourages you to grow and thrive in any situation. Through the development of these skills, you can confidently navigate the chaos. Empowerment strengthens your sense of self-worth because you finally learn what you are made of and become brave enough to ask for what you want. This ability to stand up for yourself and what you deserve, even through the challenges, will lead to a happy and successful life. This newfound courage enables you to advocate for your needs and aspirations, fostering a sense of fulfillment and achievement. Ultimately, empowerment is the key to unlocking a life that is both meaningful and richly satisfying.

Rosa Parks, the "mother of the civil rights movement," empowered herself and others when she refused to give up her seat to a white person on a segregated bus in Montgomery, Alabama, in 1955! Her defiance inspired the civil rights movement in the United States.

Malala Yousafzai, a Pakistani activist who, at just fifteen years-old, survived an assassination attempt by the Taliban, is another example of empowerment. Her remarkable story unfolds against the backdrop of her home region in Swat Valley, Pakistan, where she defied the Taliban's ban on girls' education by advocating for their right to attend school. The challenges she faced were not just physical and emotional, but ideological. She courageously stood up against a repressive regime that sought to silence her voice. Despite the attempt on her life, Malala's unwavering commitment to education and equality have made her story truly extraordinary.

She and her father cofounded the Malala Fund, which is a nonprofit organization advocating for girls' education globally. It empowers girls by advocating for their right to quality education as well as providing resources and support to ensure they can access schooling safely. The foundation has funded the building of schools in rural communities in Pakistan and advocates for policy changes around the globe. The Malala Fund has helped thousands of girls overcome barriers to education, offering them hope and opportunity for a brighter and more fulfilling future.

R*E*A*L REFLECTIONS

A = Autonomy

Autonomy and Personal Freedom

By its simplest definition, autonomy is a person's ability to act on his or her own will without external pressure or influence. Autonomy means being willing and able to make decisions for yourself. While it is a skill necessary for becoming independent, interdependency is also one of the essential building blocks to developing autonomy. Interdependency helps build autonomy by providing support and promoting healthy boundaries. When people support each other, they create a safety net that allows everyone to take risks and grow. This support boosts self-esteem and fosters mutual respect since everyone feels seen, heard, valued, and understood. Autonomy then thrives because individuals can confidently pursue their goals knowing they have a reliable foundation to fall back on if things go wrong. This balance of independence and interdependence helps people develop their own strengths.

Steve Jobs, the cofounder of Apple Inc., is celebrated as a visionary who helped shape the future of technology. By working independently and then sharing his groundbreaking ideas, he revolutionized the computer, music, phone, and animated film industries. His innovations, like the iPhone, iPod, iPad, and Pixar Animation Studios, along with his ability to anticipate consumer desires, exemplify his autonomy as both an entrepreneur and an innovator.

Jobs embodied autonomy through his unconventional approach and steadfast commitment to his vision. Unwilling to conform to norms or be controlled by external pressures, he trusted his own ideas. Jobs pursued them with unyielding passion even when he wasn't certain he would succeed. This autonomy allowed him to make bold decisions and transform industries. His legacy illustrates how trusting one's vision and having the courage to act on it can lead to trailblazing achievements.

L = Extraordinary Living

The Art of Creating Your Extraordinary Life

CHAPTER 1: R*E*A*L*

Extraordinary living means seizing the opportunity to pursue and follow your dreams so you can achieve your goals and design the life for which you yearn. It is a life lived on your terms despite challenges or naysayers. Extraordinary living means being bold enough to ask for what you want from life and then being bold enough to go and get it.

J.K. Rowling was a struggling single parent living on welfare before her books became international bestsellers. Despite facing twelve rejections from publishers, she persisted. Her determination and creativity led to the *Harry Potter* book series, which became a global phenomenon. Rowling became one of the wealthiest authors in the world, building the life of her dreams and creating a life of joy for others through her philanthropy.

> *A fear of the unknown keeps a lot of people from leaving bad situations.*
>
> — Kathie Lee Gifford

Extraordinary living needn't just happen for the sacred few; it can happen for anyone willing to step into fear. R*E*A*L* transformation comes from being bold enough to ask yourself what you really want. While you may fear that whatever lies ahead is out of your control and worry you won't have what you need to get yourself through it, you must learn to believe in yourself. You must learn to count on you, to trust that whatever comes will only serve to make you more of who you really are. If you let it, fear will keep you from living the life you have been created to live, and there can be no extraordinary living from the shadows. So I hope that, if not today, sometime in the very near future you'll …

> *Promise me you'll always remember: You're braver than you believe, and stronger than you seem, and smarter than you think.*
>
> — A. A. Milne

CHAPTER 1: R*E*A*L*

Extraordinary living means seizing the opportunity to pursue and follow your dreams so you can achieve your goals and design the life for which you yearn. It is a life lived on your terms despite challenges or naysayers. Extraordinary living means being bold enough to ask for what you want from life and then being bold enough to go and get it.

J.K. Rowling was a struggling single parent living on welfare before her books became international bestsellers. Despite facing twelve rejections from publishers, she persisted. Her determination and creativity led to the *Harry Potter* book series, which became a global phenomenon. Rowling became one of the wealthiest authors in the world, building the life of her dreams and creating a life of joy for others through her philanthropy.

> *A fear of the unknown keeps a lot of people from leaving bad situations.*
>
> — Kathie Lee Gifford

Extraordinary living needn't just happen for the sacred few; it can happen for anyone willing to step into fear. R*E*A*L* transformation comes from being bold enough to ask yourself what you really want. While you may fear that whatever lies ahead is out of your control and worry you won't have what you need to get yourself through it, you must learn to believe in yourself. You must learn to count on you, to trust that whatever comes will only serve to make you more of who you really are. If you let it, fear will keep you from living the life you have been created to live, and there can be no extraordinary living from the shadows. So I hope that, if not today, sometime in the very near future you'll …

> *Promise me you'll always remember: You're braver than you believe, and stronger than you seem, and smarter than you think.*
>
> — A. A. Milne

Chapter 2

Resilience: Bouncing Back Stronger

From Spark to Fire

Resilience, to me, is the unwavering strength and determination to confront challenges head-on, adapt to adversity, and bounce back from setbacks stronger than before. It's the ability to find the courage to keep going, even when faced with seemingly insurmountable obstacles, and to transform hardships into opportunities for growth and learning. Resilience is not just about enduring difficulties; it's about embracing them as part of the journey and using them as stepping stones toward personal development and a better future.

Sometimes, when you're in the middle of the muck, you aren't able to recognize how resilient you truly are. Throughout my life, I have cultivated resilience. For a long time, my ex-husband repeatedly told me that I wasn't smart enough to go back to school for an advanced degree. He said I wasn't capable of handling the workload. All I heard was that I wasn't enough. To be honest, school had always been a bit of a struggle, so it was easy for me to believe him. It was pounded into my head so often that it became my belief, too. I stopped even thinking about going back to school.

R*E*A*L REFLECTIONS

However, after I left that marriage, I realized that not only had my interests evolved, I needed a new set of skills. Additional education became a necessity, not just a dream. I changed jobs and met people who not only valued me but supported my desire to be more. The spark was lit, but the fire didn't begin burning right away. I knew I wanted to go back to school, but I didn't have the courage to commit fully to a doctorate. So I took baby steps and obtained a master's degree.

Have you ever wanted to do something big with your life or go somewhere out of your comfort zone only to hear that you're not smart enough, not wise enough, not brave enough, not rich enough, not skinny enough? Every time you tried to dream, someone told you that *you* just weren't enough. Maybe it was only one person's words that knocked you down. And maybe another person's words will be enough to light your fire. One person's words knocked me down, and then one person's words ignited the spark that changed the trajectory of my life. My ex-husband told me I wasn't smart enough … little did he know. Dr. Fred, my new husband, had a very different view.

A little birdie got in my ear … actually, it was Dr. Fred, my fantastic and wonderful husband … and he wasn't in my ear, we were standing in our kitchen. We were chatting (once again) about how the company I worked for was offering tuition reimbursement. I had already completed my master's degree (with lots of trials, tribulation, and hard work). And while I had enjoyed going back to school, I felt like I was finished! So when the topic of me going back to school for a doctorate came up—again—I was armed with my usual response: "I'm not smart enough. I'm too old to go back to school. What difference does it make?" Dr. Fred went quiet. When I looked up, for the very first time, I saw anger in his eyes. Before he could stop himself, he blurted out, "Are you out of your mind!?" But when he saw the look on my face, his whole body and voice softened, and he reminded me of my worth, value, and ability. "Of course you are smart enough! Of course you are wise enough! You are *not* too old, and it matters a lot! You should, you can, and you will be successful in this. You will be Dr. Teri! I believe in you." And with those words from Fred, my cheerleader, my spark began to glow a little brighter.

Despite all the years I was told I wasn't smart enough, and armed with a newfound fire in my belly and books of quotes from famous people, I was driven to

CHAPTER 2 : RESILIENCE

pursue my doctorate in special education. Through relentless challenges, effort, perseverance, and a lot of work dismantling my negative beliefs about myself, I overcame. I proved to myself that not only could I earn a doctorate degree, I could use that degree to help create powerful positive changes in the world around me. Resilience became my superpower. And it can become yours, too!

The next section is full of quotes that helped to stir the fire in my soul as I was working through not only my doctorate, but the challenges of life. I encourage you to allow these words into your heart and soul. Perhaps they won't mean to you what they mean to me, but that's okay. Allow them to help you see yourself in a new light and redefine the roads you have traveled that brought you here.

After each quote, there is space for you to write down your thoughts, feelings, goals, and dreams or just doodle—whatever helps you tap into your resilience. Reflect on times in your life when you overcame, when you were maybe too deep in the muck to notice how incredible it was that you made it out. There are also keywords and questions for reflection that may help you.

Embracing Vulnerability as Strength

Too often in life, you look behind rather than looking forward. Think about what it is that you want moving forward. Consider how all of your experiences have contributed to who you are today and how this knowledge can positively influence your future.

Once you choose hope,
anything's possible.

— Christopher Reeve

Keyword for reflection: Hope

› What gives you hope?
› What circumstances in your life made you lose hope?

Yesterday is ashes,
tomorrow wood.
Only today does the fire
burn brightly. Live today!

— Inuit proverb

Keyword for reflection: Mindfulness

› How can you be present in the day that is today?
› What can you do just for today to pay attention to the details of your extraordinary life?
› Take a moment to sit quietly somewhere today and write down everything you see around you.

It's your outlook on life that counts. If you take yourself lightly and don't take yourself too seriously, pretty soon you can find the humor in our everyday lives. And sometimes it can be a lifesaver.

— Betty White

Keyword for reflection: Humor

› When was the last time you laughed?
› When was the last time you played?
› What does it mean to take life too seriously?

Be happy in the
moment, that is enough.
Each moment is all we need,
not more.

— Saint Teresa of Calcutta

Keyword for reflection: Happiness

› What does happiness mean to you?
› What does it look like?
› When was the last time you felt happy?

R*E*A*L REFLECTIONS

CHAPTER 2 : RESILIENCE

I met Joanne at an educational conference in Cape Town, South Africa.

Joanne was a new teacher who loved her job with all her heart. She knew that education was a lifeline for her students, giving them a chance to escape poverty and dream of a better future. In a country with limited opportunities, her classroom was a safe place where children could hope and learn.

One day, disaster struck. A devastating natural disaster tore through the area, completely destroying her school. There was no money to rebuild; it seemed like her students' educations might come to an abrupt end. Joanne felt a crushing weight on her heart. She knew how much these children needed school. Without it, their sense of safety was at risk. Their dreams of a better life could shatter, and they might be trapped in poverty forever.

Joanne wasn't ready to give up. With fire in her heart, she rallied her fellow teachers, parents, and even some of the children to create a safe learning space. Using whatever scraps they could find—wooden planks, tarps, and scrap metal—they built makeshift classrooms. It wasn't much, but it was enough to keep hope alive.

Conditions were challenging! Rain leaked through the tarps, and the wind blew through the gaps. But everyday, Joanne and her colleagues poured their hearts into teaching despite the tough conditions. Joanne's determination shone like a beacon, inspiring everyone around her. Her resilience and unwavering belief in the power of education touched the hearts of the whole community.

The makeshift classrooms became a symbol of their strength and unity. Through sheer determination, they proved that nothing could stop them from dreaming. Joanne's story is a reminder that, even in the darkest times, the human spirit can transform despair to hope against all odds.

You may never know what results come from your actions, but if you do nothing, there will be no results.

— Mahatma Gandhi

Keyword for reflection: Action

› What action can you take right now to chip away at a challenge?
› What are some things that you can do to shift despair to hope?

Keep your face to the sunshine and you cannot see a shadow.

— Helen Keller

Keyword for reflection: Belief

› Do you believe that you are resilient?
› What challenges have you overcome already in your life?

Successful people maintain a positive focus in life no matter what is going on around them. They stay focused on their past successes rather than their past failures, and on the next action steps they need to take to get them closer to the fulfillment of their goals rather than all the other distractions that life presents to them.

— Jack Canfield

Keyword for reflection: Success

› What does success look like to you?
› Who or what inspires you?
› Who do you inspire?

To succeed, you need to find something to hold onto, something to motivate you, something to inspire you.

— Tony Dorsett

Keyword for reflection: Motivation

› What motivates you?
› What one thing can you do today to motivate yourself?

R*E*A*L REFLECTIONS

CHAPTER 2 : RESILIENCE

I met Joe at a gala in Washington, D.C.

Joe had been on track to compete at the Olympic Games. But a training accident changed everything, and, despite efforts to save his leg, it was amputated. This devastating turn of events shattered Joe's dreams and tested his spirit in ways he never imagined.

During his rehabilitation, swimming sessions reignited Joe's competitive spirit. It was through these tough sessions that his resilience began to shine. He refused to let his accident define him or his future. After many months of intense rehab and training, Joe qualified for the Paralympic Games. Seeing other Paralympic events inspired him to try running again, and he was soon fitted with a running prosthesis.

At the next Paralympic Games, Joe set an American long-jump record and won a silver medal. Reflecting on his journey, he said, "I did not overcome the loss of my limb. What I overcame were the limits I placed on myself and that others placed on me. This is what is universal for all of us to overcome."

Joe's story is a testament to resilience. His ability to adapt and find new dreams after such a life-changing event is inspiring. Resilience isn't just about bouncing back; it's about finding the strength to pursue new paths and redefine success. After his athletic career, Joe joined the U.S. Olympic and Paralympic Committee and started the Paralympic Military Program, helping thousands of service members find new hope and purpose through sports. Joe's journey shows that resilience can transform one's own life and inspire others to overcome obstacles and pursue their passions. Success wears many hats and often doesn't look the way we expect it to look. Joe is a perfect example of this!

The real test is not whether you avoid this failure, because you won't. It's whether you let it harden or shame you into inaction, or whether you learn from it; whether you choose to persevere.

— Barack Obama

Keyword for reflection: Failure

› What failure do you fear?
› What do you believe this failure says about you?

When you are
enthusiastic about
what you do,
you feel this
positive energy.
It's very simple.

— Paulo Coelhor

Keyword for reflection: Enthusiasm

› What do you feel enthusiastic about?
› What can you do today to ignite some of that enthusiasm?

_____
_____
_____
_____
_____
_____
_____
_____
_____
_____
_____
_____
_____
_____
_____
_____
_____
_____
_____
_____
_____
_____
_____
_____
_____
_____
_____

The only way
to do great work
is to love what
you do. If you
haven't found
it yet, keep looking.
Don't settle.

— Steve Jobs

Keyword for reflection: Passion

› Do you love what you do?
› If not, why aren't you doing what you love?

I realized early on that success was tied to not giving up. Most people in this business gave up and went on to other things. If you simply didn't give up, you would outlast the people who came in on the bus with you.

— Harrison Ford

Keyword for reflection: Persistence

› Have you given up?
› Why?
› What does persistence mean to you?

_____

R*E*A*L REFLECTIONS

CHAPTER 2 : RESILIENCE

I met Emily at a fundraising event.

After her husband's sudden and unexpected death, Emily was left with the daunting task of raising four young children, all under the age of ten, alone. The grief was overwhelming, and though her family tried to support her, they couldn't fully grasp the depths of her despair. She felt lost and consumed by sadness.

However, Emily knew she had to push through for her children. Their well-being became her driving force. Despite the pain, she found small moments of strength in her daily routines with them. She moved forward for their sake. Gradually, Emily reached out to other families who had suffered similar losses. She started attending local support groups, where she met parents who truly understood her pain. These meetings became a lifeline, offering her a space to share her grief and find comfort.

Seeing how much these connections helped, Emily decided to create a formal support network for families like hers. She organized regular gatherings for families to share their stories and support each other. They held activities for the children, allowing them to play and heal together. The network also provided counseling sessions, workshops on coping strategies, and a helpline for immediate support.

Through this process, Emily found her own path to healing. She saw the difference her network made in the lives of others and felt a renewed sense of purpose. Today, Emily is doing much better. Though she still misses her husband deeply, she has found strength in helping others. Her children are growing up in a community filled with love and understanding, knowing they are not alone in their grief. Emily's journey from despair to hope shows how resilience and compassion can create powerful change.

Turn your wounds into wisdom.

—Oprah Winfrey

Keyword for reflection: Wisdom

› What are your wounds?
› Have your wounds brought you to a place of deeper insight?
› How do you define wisdom?
› Where do you find wisdom?

Rock bottom became the solid foundation on which I rebuilt my life.

— J.K. Rowling

Keyword for reflection: Despondent

› Have you experienced being at rock bottom?
› What does this mean to you?
› What does it mean to start again?

I've missed more than 9000 shots in my career. I've lost almost 300 games. Twenty-six times I've been trusted to take the game-winning shot and missed. I've failed over and over and over again in my life. And that is why I succeed.

— Michael Jordan

Keyword for reflection: Endurance

› Do you judge yourself or others harshly for failing?
› What is an example of a failure that can become an opportunity for your growth and endurance? How?

She stood in
the storm, and
when the wind
did not blow her
away, she adjusted
her sails.

— Elizabeth Edwards

Keyword for reflection: Adapt

› How do you respond to change?
› Do you consider yourself to be flexible?

R*E*A*L REFLECTIONS

Practicing Resilience Daily

Now that you recognize that you have fire in your belly, that you *are* a resilient being, here are four practices to build your resilience muscle and make it one of your superpowers! In addition to reading quotes and journaling each day, I take part in these activities. You don't have to do all of these practices at the same time, but regular engagement with them will support your growth.

Mindfulness and Meditation

Engaging in mindfulness exercises and meditation can help you develop self-awareness, manage stress, and cultivate a sense of calm. They increase self-awareness by encouraging you to observe your thoughts and feelings without judgment. This heightened awareness then allows you to manage stress more effectively and approach situations with a clearer mind. Regular practice of mindfulness and meditation enhances emotional regulation and coping skills, contributing to greater resilience.

Practicing intentional breathing is an optimal mindfulness exercise. Set aside five minutes each morning to focus on your breathing. Sit quietly, close your eyes, and take deep breaths, paying attention to the sensation of air entering and leaving your body. This practice helps calm your mind, making you more aware of your thoughts and emotions.

For meditation, explore apps like Headspace or Calm to guide you through your sessions. These apps offer various meditation techniques that can help you manage stress, improve concentration, and develop a sense of control over your body and your mind.

Strong Connections

Build and nurture healthy and strong connections with friends, family, or support groups for emotional support during challenging times. Having a network to openly share experiences and feelings reduces stress and fosters a sense of belonging. These relationships offer comfort, advice, and encouragement, making it easier to cope with difficulties and bounce back from setbacks.

Make it a habit to have dinner with your family at least once a week. Use this time to share experiences, discuss challenges, and offer support. This regular interaction strengthens familial bonds and provides a reliable support system.

You can also participate in local or online support groups related to your interests or challenges. For instance, if you're dealing with grief, join a grief support group to connect with others who can understand your experience and provide mutual support.

Goal Setting and Problem Solving

Set achievable goals, both short-term and long-term. This provides a sense of purpose and direction, making it easier to stay motivated and focused. Developing problem-solving skills will help you navigate obstacles effectively, boosting your confidence to tackle challenges with grace. This proactive approach to life builds resilience by reinforcing your ability to adapt and persevere.

Short-term: Set small, attainable goals, such as finishing a book or learning a new recipe each week. Achieving these goals gives you a sense of accomplishment and motivates you to pursue larger objectives.

Long-term: Plan long-term goals, like earning a degree or starting a new career. Break down these goals into manageable steps and celebrate each milestone. This process keeps you focused and provides a clear direction for your efforts.

Exercise

Exercise has many benefits for your mental and physical well-being. It releases endorphins, which reduces stress and improves mood. It also strengthens your body, giving you the energy needed to face challenges. By maintaining a routine of regular exercise, you build a foundation of health and vitality that supports your overall resilience.

R*E*A*L REFLECTIONS

Take a thirty-minute walk each day, whether it's around your neighborhood or in a local park. This simple exercise improves your mood, reduces stress, and increases your energy levels.

If you want more engagement or company, try joining a fitness class, like yoga, Pilates, or spinning. Regular participation not only enhances your physical health but also provides a social outlet and a sense of community.

Through these practices, you'll grow and strengthen your own resilience!

Chapter 3

Empowerment: Transforming from Within

The True Meaning of Personal Power

My ex-husband wore me down, leaving me feeling broken and powerless throughout our marriage. But, as I stood backed-up against the cabinet in the kitchen while he raged at me that I was an incompetent and terrible mother, threatened to take our daughter because I didn't cut her potatoes the right way, and mocked me for being incapable of making a decision, I did make a decision. A big one. I decided to leave and not look back. Of course, he said things would get better, but I had had enough. I wanted to be able to make decisions. I wanted the freedom to go and do things. I *needed* to remember the person I was before all of that. I had made my first independent decision … and, with that, I made self-empowerment one of my superpowers.

As I packed up our belongings, loaded my car, left my beloved dog, Bushi, behind, enrolled my daughter in a new school, and navigated custody, I began to rely on my own inner resources. I was finally finding my voice, my empowered self, as I overcame obstacle after obstacle. I proved to myself (and to my former spouse) that not only was I capable of moving on, I could do so without his help.

R*E*A*L REFLECTIONS

Although I was successfully handling the immediate, day-to-day demands of starting a new life, of escaping, I recognized that I still needed to dig deeper to really flourish. The emotional abuse had stripped away my confidence and left me feeling trapped and alone, a shadow of myself. Despite the pain, I found the resilience to go back to school. Education became my refuge, a place where I could rebuild my sense of self and gain the knowledge I needed to reclaim my life. Every class I attended, every exam I passed, was a step toward regaining my strength and independence.

Dr. Fred's unwavering support was crucial during this time. He constantly reminded me of my worth and encouraged me to believe in myself. His belief in me was the catalyst I needed to start seeing my own power. As I became more aware of how resilient I had been throughout my life, I acted with more courage in my decisions. I learned to calmly and confidently stand up for myself and use my voice.

Recognizing and stepping into my empowerment was one of the greatest gifts I ever gave myself. It was transformative to realize that I had the strength to make my own choices. It wasn't easy, but I've learned that nothing worth having ever is. The harder you work for something, the more deeply you appreciate it.

My journey from resilience to empowerment taught me that true power comes from within. It comes from recognizing my worth, standing up for myself, and daring to demand better for my life. And while the road was filled with challenges, it was also filled with the profound realization that I had the strength to overcome them.

And so do you!

In the next section are quotes that helped to stir the fire in my soul when I decided to demand and go through with a divorce. I encourage you to allow these words into your heart and soul. Perhaps they won't mean to you what they mean to me, but that's okay. Allow them to help you see yourself and your emancipation in a new light.

After each quote, you'll have space to write down your thoughts, feelings, goals, and dreams or just doodle—whatever helps you to reflect on your own power. There are also keywords and questions to facilitate your reflections.

Finding Your Voice

Are you still looking over your shoulder, thinking about what has been rather than what can be? It's time to embody the present moment, to fully live the life you are in. It is time to believe in yourself. Allow yourself to truly dream, to think big. What is it that you want moving forward? Think about who you really are … deep down inside! Think about how all of your experiences have already positively influenced you and how they can help you to create your future.

Remember, the past is a chapter in your book, but it is not the whole story. Each page you've turned, every challenge you've faced, and all the triumphs you've celebrated have built the resilient, resourceful person you are today. Embrace the lessons learned and the strength gained as you move forward. Your future is a blank canvas ready for you to paint with the colors of your dreams and aspirations. Let go of the weight of what was, and step boldly into what can be with confidence and a heart open to endless possibilities. You have the power to create the life you want—one filled with purpose, joy, and fulfillment. So take that first step, dream big, and believe in the amazing future that lies ahead.

Start by doing what's necessary; then do what's possible; and suddenly you are doing the impossible.

— Unknown

Keyword for reflection: Start!

› What have you been waiting for? To start?

It takes courage
to grow up and
become who
you really are.

— E. E. Cummings

Keyword for reflection: Soul-searching

› Which parts of yourself have you been hiding from the world?
› Why are you afraid to let them be seen?

Nothing is impossible.
The word itself
says I'M POSSIBLE.

— Audrey Hepburn

Keyword for reflection: Self-trust

› What accomplishments in your life are you proud of?
› Do you trust that you have what it takes to overcome challenges?

If you don't like
something, change it.
If you can't change it,
change your attitude.
Don't complain.

— Maya Angelou

Keyword for reflection: Ownership

› Are you afraid to take responsibility for your life?
› Why?

R*E*A*L REFLECTIONS

CHAPTER 3 : EMPOWERMENT

I met Carl in a financial education meeting.

Carl grew up in a home where money was always tight, and he didn't have anyone to teach him how to manage finances properly. As a hardworking single dad later in life, he faced a lot of financial challenges and felt a huge responsibility to do right by his children. The constant stress of not having enough money weighed heavily on him.

Not only did Carl not have much money, he also struggled with making good decisions about it. He often found himself in debt, worried about how to make ends meet, and felt like he was failing his children. The nights were long and filled with anxiety. Determined to break the cycle and set a positive example for them, Carl decided to take control of his financial situation and learn about money management.

Since he couldn't afford a financial advisor, Carl turned to the free adult education classes in his town. He signed up for courses taught by finance experts and soaked up everything he could about budgeting, saving, and investing. He asked tons of questions, stayed late after class, and pushed himself to really understand the material, determined to put what he learned into practice.

With persistence and hard work, Carl started making better financial decisions. He practiced budgeting and saving, slowly building a more stable financial foundation for his family. The relief and pride he felt as he saw progress were overwhelming. He knew he was creating a better future.

Carl's efforts modeled the importance of financial literacy and resilience. He taught his children that with determination and education, they, too, could overcome challenges and achieve long-term success.

> Perpetual
> optimism
> is a force
> multiplier.
>
> — Colin Powell

Keyword for reflection: Optimism

› In what areas of your life are you most optimistic?
› How does this optimism impact your relationships with others?

If you can
dream it,
you can
do it.

— Walt Disney

Keyword for reflection: Vision

› A vision is powerful; do you ever envision a different version of yourself?
› What does this person look like?

Start where you are. Use what you have. Do what you can.

— Arthur Ashe

Keyword for reflection: Initiative

› What actions can you take toward your goals regardless of your circumstances?
› How can you challenge your own excuses for inaction?

If you don't make the time to work on creating the life you want, you're eventually going to be forced to spend a lot of time dealing with a life you don't want.

— Kevin Ngo

Keyword for reflection: Self-rescue

› What are your thoughts on coming to your own rescue?
› Do you blame others for the way your life is? Who and why?
› How can you take action to move forward with your dreams?

R*E*A*L REFLECTIONS

CHAPTER 3 : EMPOWERMENT

I met Brian at a hospital fundraising event.

Brian dropped out of high school after just three years of attendance, feeling that formal schooling wasn't for him. He decided to join the military and served his country for six years. During his service, he learned practical skills, discipline, and teamwork while discovering his own strength and resilience.

After being honorably discharged, Brian realized there was still so much more he wanted to do with his life and decided to get his GED (General Educational Development). He knew that further education was the key to reaching his goals. Empowering himself, he enrolled in community college courses focusing on healthcare and earned his certification and licensure.

Brian's hard work paid off, and he began working in a hospital, where he used his skills to help hundreds of people every day. The lessons he learned in the military, like handling tough situations and caring for others, were invaluable in his new role. As a wonderful bonus, Brian met and married the love of his life while working at the hospital.

By empowering himself through education and trusting in his abilities, Brian was able to make a significant impact on the lives of others. His journey from high school dropout to a dedicated healthcare worker shows how believing in oneself and taking bold steps can help break through limitations and make anything happen.

Setting goals is
the first step
in turning the
invisible into
the visible.

— Tony Robbins

Keyword for reflection: Goals

› How do you define a goal?
› Do you have goals? If so, what are they?
› What small steps can you take this week to move yourself toward these goals?

The start is what stops
most people.

— Don Shula

Keyword for reflection: Fear

› What do you fear?
› Do you see fear as weakness?
› How do you respond to fear?

Great minds have purposes, others have wishes. Little minds are tamed and subdued by misfortunes; but great minds rise above them.

— Washington Irving

Keyword for reflection: Purpose

› What do you think of the statement, "Purpose propels you through misfortune"?
› What do you think your purpose is?

The best
revenge is
massive success.

— Frank Sinatra

Keyword for reflection: Self-confidence

› Are there people in your life who have told you that you will never achieve your dreams?
› What do you say to the naysayers?

R*E*A*L REFLECTIONS

CHAPTER 3 : EMPOWERMENT

I met Jamie and Marco through a parenting group.

Jamie and Marco are parents who faced many healthcare system hurdles because their son has serious physical and cognitive challenges. At first, they were scared and stressed about his future and felt lost trying to get him the care he needed. They spent many days in hospitals while battling insurance companies that often denied them help. It was a tough and traumatic time.

Instead of giving up, Jamie and Marco decided to fight for better healthcare and social services. They turned their fear into action and talked to local policymakers. They shared their personal struggles, highlighting how hard it was for families like theirs to navigate the healthcare system. They found out that many other families were going through the same thing.

Their efforts paid off. By telling their story, they made more people aware of the need for better healthcare resources and support for families like theirs. Policymakers listened, and soon there were real changes, like more funding for healthcare programs and better training for medical staff.

Jamie and Marco also created an online support group for parents all over the world. This group helped families connect, share their stories, and support each other. It became a place where parents could find comfort and advice from others who understood their struggles.

Jamie's and Marco's story shows that standing up for yourself can lead to tangible transformation. They turned their tough experiences into a way to help others, improving the healthcare system and demonstrating the power of advocacy and empowerment.

I'm not going to limit myself just because people won't accept the fact that I can do something else.

— Dolly Parton

Keyword for reflection: Tenacity

› What are some words you use to describe yourself?
› Can you name two situations where you believed in yourself and what the result of that self-belief was?

If I cannot do
great things, I
can do small things
in a great way.

— Martin Luther King Jr.

Keyword for reflection: Consequential

› Empowering yourself doesn't always have to look like reformed policies and radical life transformation—sometimes it's as simple as saying no. When did you last say no?
› What other small but *great* things have you accomplished?

When everything seems to be going against you, remember that the airplane takes off against the wind, not with it.

— Henry Ford

Keyword for reflection: Patience

› Would others describe you as a patient person? Why or why not?
› How can you practice more patience today?

When your clarity meets your conviction and you apply action to the equation, your world will begin to transform before your eyes.

— Lisa Nichols

Keyword for reflection: Progress

› What does your first step look like?
› How do you imagine feeling after you take it?

R*E*A*L REFLECTIONS

Empowerment Through Action: Persistence and Determination

Now that you recognize that you are an empowered being, here are four practices to strengthen your empowerment muscle and make it one of your superpowers! In addition to reading quotes and journaling each day, I take part in these activities. You don't have to do all of these practices at the same time, but engaging in them regularly will reinforce your empowerment.

Self-reflection

Regularly spend time self-reflecting. This gives you the opportunity to understand and build upon your strengths, think about and improve your weaknesses, and envision and act on your values and aspirations. Honor and accept yourself—the good, the bad, and the ugly!

Journaling and meditation are two very practical ways to practice self-reflection. Set aside time each day to write about your experiences, feelings, and thoughts. Focus on specific situations where you felt you used your strengths or encountered challenges. Spend time in quiet contemplation and focus on what went well, what didn't, and why. Think about your thoughts and feelings without judgment. Over time, review your entries to identify patterns and insights.

Self-compassion

Practice self-compassion and positive self-talk. These will build your confidence and self-worth. Try the following mantras for positive self-talk:

- I am enough just as I am.
- I choose to be kind to myself.
- Every day, in every way, I am getting better and better.
- I am worthy of love and respect.
- I am resilient, strong, and capable.
- I embrace my flaws and celebrate my strengths.

CHAPTER 3 : EMPOWERMENT

- I am in control of my thoughts and emotions.
- I forgive myself for past mistakes and learn from them.
- I trust myself and my decisions.
- I am deserving of happiness and success.

Embrace Knowledge

Expand your knowledge in areas that interest you. Try new things! You might do this through formal education, online courses, workshops, or self-study. Cultivating a new area of expertise reinforces your confidence so that you can tackle new challenges and create more opportunities for your future.

Express Yourself

This is a BIGGIE! Learn to express your thoughts, feelings, and needs assertively and respectfully. It is okay to say no, especially to Negative Nellies. A Negative Nelly is someone who consistently has a pessimistic attitude. They focus on problems and potential failures rather than opportunities. They complain, criticize, lack enthusiasm, and expect the worst outcomes. In your life, a Negative Nelly might be a coworker who doubts the success of projects, a friend who dismisses positive experiences, or a family member who never has a nice thing to say. Their constant negativity can be draining and demotivating, impacting your mood and outlook. Recognizing these individuals and setting boundaries with them can help protect your energy and your perspectives.

When you set boundaries, like saying no when necessary or standing up for yourself in a calm and confident manner, you let people know that they can't take advantage of you.

Self-empowerment is an ongoing process that involves self-awareness, confidence-building, and taking small, consistent, proactive steps toward personal growth and fulfillment.

YOU are an empowered being!

Chapter 4
Autonomy in Action

The Power of Making Your Own Choices

Having autonomy and being autonomous means that you have the power and the freedom to make decisions for yourself, to do what you feel is best for you, and to have the independence to do so without question. It means that no one else needs to tell you what you should do or what is right for you. Autonomy means that you have control over your life and how you respond to what goes on around you.

It was important for me to establish and protect my autonomy, not only for myself but for my daughter. I needed to make decisions independently about what I thought was right for us, for our safety, and for our emotional, mental, and financial health. But, even more importantly, I needed to model this skill (and, yes, it is a skill) so that my daughter could see that she, too, had the freedom to make choices and decisions, to be independent, and to take control of her life. I didn't want her to lose herself to someone else like I had.

When I was a child, I was extraordinarily independent. While I depended on my parents and the other caring adults in my life for the essentials, I was perfectly happy to do most things by myself. I was bold to say the least! My mom would often find me climbing to the top of a tree to watch for the bullies in the neighborhood or walking into the swamp to gather the cattails so we could light them around the fire. I was the one who swam across the lake through the lily pads and the weeds … just because I could.

But when I got married the first time, I slowly became overly-dependent on my spouse without even realizing it. The shift from independence to dependence can happen gradually and subtly. Initially, it seemed natural to lean on my partner; it felt like love and trust, support and guidance. My reliance turned into dependency as I began to doubt myself and feel anxious about making mistakes. Eventually, I lost confidence in my own decision-making abilities. Insecurity, fear of failure, and a desire for approval drove me to lean more heavily on my partner, creating a cycle of dependence. Whenever I made a decision, it felt wrong, no doubt because he would often tell me it was wrong, which further eroded my self-esteem and trust in my abilities. So I stopped making decisions altogether, as it felt safer to rely entirely on him. Over time, inadequacy and loneliness dominated my life, making me feel disconnected from my own identity and lacking in autonomy. Ultimately, I didn't like who I had become, but I felt trapped and unsure of how to regain my independence.

Breaking free from this cycle meant facing those same emotions that had driven me to dependency. Determination to rediscover myself and regain my independence became a powerful motivator. Courage to face the fear of failure head-on and accept that mistakes are part of the learning process was crucial. Learning self-compassion and forgiving my past mistakes helped rebuild my confidence. In the face of fear, I found strength within myself to become autonomous, making crucial decisions not just for me but also for my daughter, ensuring our physical and emotional safety. Each small decision I made on my own, whether right or wrong, began to restore my sense of self and autonomy, empowering me to move forward.

Taking charge of my finances was an empowering journey. When I left, I took very little from our home, so building a household from scratch tested my resolve. It involved careful planning and prioritizing essentials, teaching me to

CHAPTER 4 : AUTONOMY

manage money effectively. One of my first steps was creating a budget so that I could track every expense. Every bill I paid became a symbol of my newfound self-reliance. Buying a car on my own proved that I could not just survive but thrive independently. I emerged stronger, demonstrating that I could create a secure life for myself and my daughter despite the chaos.

I educated myself about personal finance through books. Opening my own bank accounts and setting financial goals gave me direction and accountability. I also sought advice from financial advisors to understand investments and retirement planning.

Throughout this journey, I experienced many emotions. Determination drove me to provide a stable environment for my daughter and me. Fear and uncertainty were constant companions as I managed finances alone, but each successful step filled me with pride and a sense of accomplishment. Gaining financial independence made me feel empowered and in control of my future. This journey turned fear and uncertainty into strength and self-reliance.

Why am I telling you this? Because everything you long for lies on the other side of everything you are afraid of!

Raising my daughter as a single parent meant that I didn't have someone looking over my shoulder. This freedom allowed me to explore my capabilities fully and make my own decisions about her upbringing. My ex and I had different views on several fundamental aspects of raising her. We disagreed on discipline methods; he favored a strict approach while I believed in a more gentle and nurturing approach.

After I left, I implemented a positive reinforcement strategy, focusing on rewarding good behavior and using mistakes as learning opportunities. I encouraged a balanced approach to learning, prioritizing both academics and activities that nurtured her emotional intelligence and creativity. I allowed my daughter to choose extracurricular activities that she genuinely enjoyed. This enabled her to develop a love for hobbies and interests that made her happy and confident. I also fostered open communication, ensuring my daughter felt heard and valued. These changes allowed me to raise my daughter in a nurturing and supportive environment that felt right to me and aligned with my values.

It was wonderful to realize that I could and should make decisions on my own terms and according to what I believed in. Initially, to my surprise, these decisions were not only valid but also respected. This was beyond liberating. Being respected for my own thoughts, decisions, and opinions affirmed my capability to navigate life's challenges with grace and determination. I started to trust myself and my competency. I embraced autonomy as another newfound superpower, emerging from the darkness of fear and doubt as an independent, confident, and intelligent woman!

The following quotes became beacons of strength and inspiration during those times when I needed to remind myself of my independence, autonomy, and ability to make my own wise choices. I encourage you to allow these words into your heart and soul. Perhaps they won't mean to you what they mean to me, but that's okay. Use this opportunity to explore your independence and discover the power that lies within you.

After each quote, there will be space for you to write down your thoughts, feelings, goals, and dreams or just doodle—express yourself in any way that helps you reflect on your autonomy. There are keywords and questions to help you explore how these quotes resonate with you personally.

Embracing Your Personal Freedom

How many times have you made a decision and been questioned about it or made to feel that you shouldn't trust your thoughts or decisions? Has someone—your partner, parents, or spouse—told you that your decisions aren't good and that you should do what they say instead?

Do you find yourself getting caught up in reflecting on your past rather than looking ahead to the future? Do you relive past experiences, ruminating on them, allowing them to define you instead of stepping into your power and actively shaping your future? It's important to imagine the life you envision for yourself and your family, recognizing that every experience you've had, whether positive or challenging, can contribute to your future journey if you allow it to.

> Education is the most powerful weapon which you can use to change the world.
>
> — Nelson Mandela

Keyword for reflection: Educate

› Do you want to go back to school or pursue a degree for the first time?
› Do you have academic goals that you have sacrificed for someone or something?
› If you could pursue any education now, what would it be?

The function of education is to teach one to think intensively and to think critically. Intelligence plus character—that is the goal of true education.

— Martin Luther King Jr.

Keyword for reflection: Self-advocate

› Are you willing to question others when you don't agree with what is being said or done?
› When they don't agree with what you believe?
› When you see something wrong happening?

I'm always asked,
"What's the secret
to success?" But there
are no secrets.
Be humble.
Be hungry.
And always be the
hardest worker in the room.

— Dwayne (The Rock) Johnson

Keyword for reflection: Humility

› What does being humble look like to you?
› Do you think being humble means being a walkover or submissive?
› What are you hungry for?

Do the one thing you think you cannot do. Fail at it. Try again. Do better the second time. The only people who never tumble are those who never mount the high wire. This is your moment. Own it.

— Oprah Winfrey

Keyword for reflection: Doubt

› What is the one thing that you think you cannot do?
› What is the worst thing that could happen if that is true?
› What is something that you are good at that you didn't think you were?

R*E*A*L REFLECTIONS

I met Kim when I went back to school myself!

Kim, an older student, was passionate about a nontraditional field of study: complementary therapies, which combines holistic health practices with conventional medicine. This unique interest made it challenging for her to find a school that could meet her wants, needs, and expectations. She faced numerous difficulties, including limited course offerings and societal expectations that often marginalized nontraditional students and unconventional academic pursuits.

Kim navigated these challenges with persistence and determination. She tirelessly researched potential schools, only to face repeated rejections. Each rejection was a blow to her confidence, leaving her feeling disheartened and questioning her path. However, her deep passion for complementary therapies kept her going. She found solace in the small victories, such as discovering a professor who shared her interest or a course that partially aligned with her goals.

Kim's commitment to her educational aspirations, coupled with her innovative insights into alternative academic routes, enabled her to propose a personalized program. With the help and blessing of a progressive college, she crafted a unique curriculum that combined courses from different departments, independent studies, and hands-on fieldwork. This individualized program was designed to fulfill both her academic requirements and her personal goals, integrating courses in nutrition, acupuncture, herbal medicine, and conventional medical practices to create a comprehensive complementary therapies curriculum.

Despite experiencing a roller coaster of emotions, Kim created her own autonomous pathway. Overcoming the frustration and isolation she felt when confronted with the rigid structures of the traditional educational system, her unwavering dedication to her dream provided her with the strength to persevere. The moments of acceptance and support she received from her college were profoundly validating, filling her with hope and determination.

By pursuing her ideas, letting go of limiting beliefs, and being willing to complete her coursework, Kim not only achieved her academic goals but also paved the way for other students with nontraditional academic endeavors. Her story is one of independence, autonomy, and innovation, demonstrating that with passion and persistence, it is possible to carve out a unique path for your future even if it means you start alone.

We all have dreams.
But in order to
make dreams come
into reality, it takes
an awful lot of
determination,
dedication, self-discipline,
and effort.

— Jesse Owens

Keyword for reflection: Courage

› Is fear of success one of the reasons you play small with your life or avoid independence?
› Is it because of the work it requires?
› Does it feel simpler to stay where you are and depend on others than to take responsibility for your own life?

Remember to look up at the stars and not down at your feet. Try to make sense of what you see and wonder about what makes the universe exist. Be curious.

— Stephen Hawking

Keyword for reflection: Curiosity

› Do you remember being curious as a child?
› What kind of activities kept you busy and engaged your imagination?
› When did you last use curiosity to explore your world?

The greatest sign of success for a teacher ... is to be able to say, "The children are now working as if I do not exist."

— Maria Montessori

Keyword for reflection: Self-reliant

› What does independence look like to you?
› What does self-reliant mean?
› If you take the training wheels off, where can you go in your life right now?

> The more things you do, the more you can do.
>
> — Lucille Ball

Keyword for reflection: Momentum

› What is something you can do on your own that will enable you to do more on your own?
› What positive habits can you cultivate to create change?

R*E*A*L REFLECTIONS

CHAPTER 4 : AUTONOMY

Annette is a former student and now my colleague.

Annette broke away from her family's expectations of choosing a career in medicine and instead pursued a career in education. Inspired by her love for working with children and her passion for fostering their growth and development, she knew that teaching was her true calling. For all four years of her undergraduate program, her family challenged her decision, expressing disappointment and concern. This lack of support often left Annette feeling isolated and unsure of herself, but her deep-seated belief in the importance of education and her desire to make a difference in children's lives kept her motivated.

Despite the emotional strain of not having her family's backing, Annette found solace and encouragement through her student teaching experiences and in the support of her peers and professors. These positive influences reaffirmed her choice and gave her the strength to persevere. Every time she saw a child's eyes light up with understanding or joy, she felt a profound sense of fulfillment and validation.

Annette enjoyed several years as a preschool teacher, where her creativity and dedication shone brightly. She continued her education, becoming qualified in several different subjects and age levels, ensuring that she would always have options for various classroom opportunities. This versatility not only broadened her career prospects but also reinforced her sense of autonomy.

Now Annette contributes to special programs for children with learning differences, using her creative skills in a way that illuminates not just her but the children she teaches. She challenged norms within her family and gradually helped them see that this is where she belongs. Today, Annette is happy, successful, and, most importantly, autonomous and independent, having proven that following one's passion can lead to a rewarding and impactful life.

Only I can
change my life.
No one can do
it for me.

— Carol Burnett

Keyword for reflection: Self-love

› What is one thing that you can change in your life that will help you to recognize your worth?
› How can you love yourself in a small way today?
› Write down three kind words that describe who you are as a person.

You must take
personal responsibility.
You cannot change
the circumstances,
the seasons, or the
wind, but you can
change yourself.

— Jim Rohn

Keyword for reflection: Self-sabotage

› Do you focus on what you can't control as an excuse to not change or become independent?
› What are things that are out of your control that you focus on?
› What things are in your control that you can change?
› Are you brave enough to take responsibility for your success and your failures?

One of the lessons that I grew up with was to always stay true to yourself and never let what somebody else says distract you from your goals.

— Michelle Obama

Keyword for reflection: Authenticity

› How can you maintain your independence when you are tempted to give up?
› What do you do when others say you should give up?
› What is your bigger picture?

Keep your face toward the sunshine and shadows will fall behind you.

— Walt Whitman

Keyword for reflection: Faith

› What does faith mean to you?
› What do you have faith in?

R*E*A*L REFLECTIONS

CHAPTER 4 : AUTONOMY

I met Mel in a yoga class.

When Mel embarked on a journey of self-discovery, he engaged in activities that aligned with his interests, like meditation and yoga. Before this journey, Mel often felt misunderstood and unappreciated in his previous social circles. He wasn't accepted because his interests and values differed significantly from those of his peers, who prioritized more conventional and mainstream activities. Mel often felt like an outsider, struggling with feelings of self-doubt and a lack of acceptance. He often conformed to others' expectations rather than being true to himself, which intensified his sense of isolation and uncertainty about his place in the world.

In his pursuit of inner peace, Mel found it in the quietness of meditation and the physicality of yoga. These practices allowed him to connect with like-minded people in a stress-free environment, free from the pressure of societal norms. The authenticity and genuineness he brought to these activities fostered connections with others who valued, accepted, understood, and appreciated him for who he truly was.

To step into his autonomy, Mel had to overcome his fear of rejection and the need for external validation. By prioritizing relationships characterized by mutual respect and shared values, he gradually became independent of other people's expectations. Through this process, Mel discovered and accepted himself, which significantly strengthened his self-belief and confidence.

The journey was not easy, but it was transformative. Mel learned to value his own needs and desires, setting boundaries that protected his well-being. This newfound autonomy allowed him to build a social circle that supported and celebrated his individuality, leading to a fulfilling and authentic life where he could thrive.

*If you don't
like the road
you're walking,
start paving
another one.*

— Dolly Parton

Keyword for reflection: Nonconformity

› Does autonomy to you mean resisting the urge to conform to society's expectations?
› In what ways have you conformed to avoid being rejected or abandoned?

Smile and let
everyone know
that today, you're
a lot stronger than
you were yesterday.

— Drake

Keyword for reflection: Strength

› What does strength look like to you?
› Where does strength come from?
› Who is one person in your life that you see as strong?

Some people want it to happen, some wish it would happen, others make it happen.

— Michael Jordan

Keyword for reflection: Practice

› What risk can you take that will positively change your life?
› Who are you waiting for?
› What things do you want to happen for, to, and because of you?

I know where I'm going and I know the truth, and I don't have to be what you want me to be. I'm free to be what I want.

— Muhammad Ali

Keyword for reflection: Genuine

› Who do you want to be?
› How do you want to be seen in this world?

_____
_____
_____
_____
_____
_____
_____
_____
_____
_____
_____
_____
_____
_____
_____
_____
_____
_____
_____
_____
_____
_____
_____
_____
_____
_____

R*E*A*L REFLECTIONS

Celebrating Your Autonomy: Living a Life True to Yourself

Building autonomy is a gradual process that involves developing self-confidence, decision-making skills, and a sense of independence. Following are three activities that can help build your autonomy. In addition to reading quotes and journaling each day, I take part in these activities. You don't have to do all of these practices at the same time, but regular engagement with them will support your growth.

Decision Making

Practice making decisions, both big and small, on your own. Start with minor choices, like what to eat on takeout night, and gradually move on to more significant decisions, like whether you are happy in your career or your relationships. Reflect on the outcomes of the minor decisions, learn from your experiences, and trust your judgment. This process builds confidence in your decision-making abilities and boosts your self-reliance.

Learning from Failure

Understand that failures and mistakes are a natural part of life. Instead of relying on others to fix your problems, approach setbacks as opportunities to learn and grow. Analyze your failures, identify what went wrong, and strategize on how to improve next time. By taking responsibility for your mistakes and learning from them, you will be less fearful about making decisions, which will strengthen your autonomy.

Serve

Getting involved in community service or volunteering for causes you are passionate about can boost your self-confidence and independence. Contributing to your community or a social cause not only helps others but also provides a sense of purpose and accomplishment, reinforcing your belief in your abilities to make a positive impact on the world.

Remember that building autonomy is a personal journey, and it's essential to be patient with yourself. You are perfectly imperfect! Celebrate your successes, no matter how small, and learn from your challenges. Over time, these activities will help you develop the confidence and self-assuredness needed to navigate life's challenges independently.

Embrace your autonomous self!

Chapter 5

Step Into Extraordinary Living

Embracing Your Unique Journey

By society's standards, my life might not seem extraordinary ... boring even. But, to me, it has been a thrilling, and sometimes scary, roller-coaster ride. When I reflect on my life, I see significance in all the roles I have played: parent, spouse, educator, entrepreneur, and writer, just to name a few. Each of these hats I wear tells a different story about my life, and I am proud to say that I have worn them well.

As a parent, I've come to appreciate the immense strength and resilience it takes to nurture, guide, and inspire children every day. Recognizing my ability to handle the ups and downs of parenthood empowers me to be a source of unwavering support and love for my family, as well as an example of a life well-lived.

Reflecting on what went wrong in my first marriage, I have learned some valuable lessons. I have discovered the power of asking for what I need and the importance of saying no. I have realized how crucial it is to recognize when relationships no longer serve you and to have the courage to walk away.

R*E*A*L REFLECTIONS

This experience taught me that I could survive and even thrive after leaving people behind.

In my marriage with Dr. Fred, I've had the opportunity to apply these lessons in a healthier and more supportive environment. I learned the significance of open communication and compromise. Fred and I work toward shared goals, but we also empower each other to grow individually. This balance has enriched our relationship, allowing us to cherish our journey together while respecting and encouraging each other's personal growth.

As an educator, I am passionate about empowering young minds, fostering creativity, and instilling a love for learning. My autonomous teaching style and curriculum choices allow me to be flexible and create meaningful experiences for my students that resonate with them as individuals. This always has a positive impact on their lives and academic journeys.

As an entrepreneur and writer, I am venturing into new territories fueled by individuality, vision, and a drive for success. My entrepreneurial endeavors and writing projects empower me to share my stories, insights, and passions with the world, making a lasting impression in my chosen industries.

Through recognizing my resilience, empowering myself in every role I undertake, fostering autonomy in my endeavors, and finding joy in each moment, I am creating my own extraordinary life. My family, too, is creating an extraordinary life together, one filled with purpose, growth, and meaningful connections. This journey is not just about achieving goals but also about embracing the beauty of the process and savoring every experience along the way. The days may seem long but the years are short—the time to create your extraordinary life is now!

In this next section are quotes that helped to stir the fire in my soul as I stepped into extraordinary living. I encourage you to allow these words into your heart and soul. These quotes may not mean to you what they mean to me, but that's okay. Just let yourself go with the flow and enjoy rediscovering YOU!

After each quote, you'll have space to write down your thoughts, feelings, goals, and dreams or just doodle—whatever helps you to examine your life. There are also keywords and questions to facilitate your reflections.

What Is Extraordinary Living?

Extraordinary living—what exactly does that mean? Everyone's definition should be different. You don't have to be famous, rich, or do grand things to live an extraordinary life. Your extraordinary life is just that: yours. My extraordinary life is the one I'm living right now. My journey has been a testament to resilience, passion, and dedication. And yours can be too … if you are open to it.

It's time to reclaim your power and craft the extraordinary life you deserve. Remember, it's not the big things in life that make it extraordinary; it's all of the small, great things put together. Embrace the daily acts of kindness, shared laughter, mutual encouragement, and unwavering support that are all around you. Each small moment of love, support, and achievement weaves together to create a tapestry of an extraordinary life that is uniquely yours. Step into your power, actively shape your future, and watch as your dreams unfold into reality. Extraordinary living starts with trusting your own instincts and believing in your ability to make the right decisions for yourself.

Sometimes, it's easy to replay past experiences over and over, letting them define who you are and sabotage your own success. Extraordinary living means envisioning the future you desire for yourself and your family and recognizing that the only thing worth fearing is a life lived too small.

If I have the belief that I can do it, I shall surely acquire the capacity to do it even if I may not have it at the beginning.

— Mahatma Gandhi

Keyword for reflection: Capable

› Do you see yourself as being capable of success?
› What does it mean to be capable?

Weeds are flowers too, once you get to know them.

— A. A. Milne

Keyword for reflection: Beauty

› Write down three beautiful things around you right now.
› Write down three beautiful things inside you.

There is only one person responsible for the quality of the life you live. That person is you.

— Jack Canfield

Keyword for reflection: Responsibility

› What excuses do you make for not following your dreams?
› What do you have a difficult time forgiving yourself for?
› Can you release this blame today and show yourself compassion?

The secret to success is good leadership, and good leadership is all about making the lives of your team members or workers better.

— Tony Dungy

Keyword for reflection: Leadership

› Do you model leadership?
› If so, how?
› If not, why not?
› Who leads you?

R*E*A*L REFLECTIONS

I met Sarah when I went on a mission trip to Guatemala during my doctoral studies.

Sarah's nonprofit organization brings essential medical aid to remote regions around the world, including rural areas in Africa, Southeast Asia, and South America. These communities often lack basic healthcare facilities; residents have little to no access to medical professionals, medications, or health education.

Sarah, a nurse in a busy but well-equipped and well-resourced hospital, first noticed this gap during a volunteer trip to Guatemala. In the remote areas she visited, she saw children suffering from preventable diseases, women facing childbirth complications without medical help, and elderly individuals living with untreated chronic conditions. Witnessing this drastic contrast stirred deep emotions within her—compassion, frustration, and a profound sense of responsibility.

Sarah was determined to make a difference and founded her nonprofit organization to bring healthcare to these underserved areas. Her passion inspired a network of volunteers, including doctors, nurses, and other healthcare professionals who share her vision and commitment.

Operating in foreign countries and in remote regions presents many challenges including transporting medical supplies to isolated areas. This can be difficult and costly. She and her volunteers often have to navigate rough terrains and extreme weather conditions. Corruption, cultural barriers, and language differences can complicate interactions, requiring sensitivity and adaptability from the team.

Despite these challenges, Sarah and her team have achieved remarkable success. Their medical camps provide vaccinations, basic treatments, and health education, significantly improving the well-being of thousands of people. They also work on long-term projects, like building clinics, training local healthcare workers, and setting up supply chains for essential medications.

Sarah's journey with her nonprofit shows that compassion and determination can transform an ordinary job into an extraordinary mission. By addressing the healthcare needs of remote regions, she has improved countless lives and

CHAPTER 5 : EXTRAORDINARY LIVING

demonstrated that one person's humanity can create a ripple effect of positive change. Her story of extraordinary living is a testament to the power of empathy and its profound impact on the world.

The quality of a
person's life is in
direct proportion
to their commitment
to excellence,
regardless of their
chosen field
of endeavor.

— Vince Lombardi

Keyword for reflection: Integrity

› What does integrity mean to you?
› Are you willing to face consequences for doing the right thing?

> You can have everything in life you want if you will just help enough other people get what they want.
>
> — Zig Ziglar

Keyword for reflection: Service

› How can you give back to the world?
› How can you follow your dreams and be of service without forsaking yourself?
› How can you be an example to help others follow their dreams?
› Who's watching you follow your dreams?

Thousands of candles can be lighted from a single candle, and the life of the candle will not be shortened. Happiness never decreases by being shared.

— the Buddha

Keyword for reflection: Exemplify

› How can you empower yourself to light the way for others to do the same?
› Are you a good role model?

There are no strangers here; only friends you haven't yet met.

— William Butler Yeats

Keyword for reflection: Relationships

› What would it take for you to have the courage to go out into the world and meet a new group of people?
› How can you open yourself to finding trust in a relationship?
› What are you afraid will happen if you open yourself to new people?

R*E*A*L REFLECTIONS

CHAPTER 5 : EXTRAORDINARY LIVING

I met Jessica when I taught at a local college.

Jessica, a retired teacher, recognized the importance of literacy in her community. Understanding that the ability to read and write is foundational to a child's education and future opportunities, she was moved by the struggles of underprivileged children who lacked access to books and educational resources. Watching these children face barriers to their academic success and future potential stirred deep emotions within her—indignation and a duty to do something about it.

Driven by these feelings, Jessica established volunteer libraries in underserved schools around her city. Her initiative began with a modest collection of donated books and a small group of volunteers. However, friends, relatives, and peers quickly rallied behind her cause, recognizing the importance of literacy and the positive impact it could have on the children's futures.

As the support grew, Jessica expanded her libraries, reaching hundreds of children across the city. The libraries became vibrant centers of learning and imagination, where children could explore new worlds through books and improve their reading skills.

One of the most inspiring results of Jessica's initiative was the involvement of young adults who took on service projects to support her cause. These young volunteers collected and donated books and helped set up new libraries. Their enthusiasm and dedication fostered a sense of community and a safe haven across the ages.

Jessica's dedication to literacy transformed her retirement years into an extraordinary chapter of giving back. By providing books to hundreds of children, she not only shaped their futures but also demonstrated that age is no barrier to creating meaningful change. Her story is a testament to the profound impact literacy has on young minds and has left a legacy that will last for generations to come. That's extraordinary living!

Do the best you can until you know better. Then when you know better, do better!

— Maya Angelou

Keyword for reflection: Excuses

› If you're reading this book, you now know better.
› And when you know better … you do better.
› Go do better.

Our greatest natural resource is the minds of our children.

— Walt Disney

Keyword for reflection: Imagination

› What advice would you give your younger self?
› What advice would your younger self give you?

Always work hard
and have fun in
what you do because
I think that's when
you're more successful.
You have to choose
to do it.

— Simone Biles

Keyword for reflection: Productivity

› When are you most productive?
› What contributes to positive productivity?
› How can you make your work more fun?

_____
_____
_____
_____
_____
_____
_____
_____
_____
_____
_____
_____
_____
_____
_____
_____
_____
_____
_____
_____
_____
_____
_____
_____
_____

With everything that has happened to you, you can either feel sorry for yourself or treat what has happened as a gift. Everything is either an opportunity to grow or an obstacle to keep you from growing. You get to choose.

— Wayne Dyer

Keyword for reflection: Choices

› What are some things that you might not have seen as gifts in the past, but, upon reflection, they truly are?
› What choice can you make today to change your story from victimhood to victor?

R*E*A*L REFLECTIONS

I worked with the Johnson family to implement my R*E*A*L* Peaceful Parenting framework.

The Johnson family faced challenges but emerged from my work with them stronger through mutual support and open communication. The parents, Lisa and Mark, were both busy working parents. Lisa worked full time as a nurse, and Mark owned and managed a small business. The demands of their careers often left little time for family bonding, and this imbalance took a toll on their children.

The Johnsons have three children: Emma, fifteen; Liam, ten; and Molly, seven. Each child reacted differently to the lack of attention and family time. Emma, the eldest, felt angry and anxious. She worried about missing out on special events. Liam struggled with his schoolwork, talked back, and refused to do his homework. Molly often acted out, seeking attention through tantrums and clinginess.

As the daily stress and strain continued, the children's challenging behaviors intensified. Emma became argumentative and often closed herself in her room. Liam had frequent temper tantrums and often sulked. Molly's tantrums grew more intense. The atmosphere at home grew increasingly tense and difficult to manage.

Recognizing they needed help, Lisa and Mark sought my assistance. After talking with them and meeting each of the children, we decided to implement the R*E*A*L* Peaceful Parenting framework. One of the first interventions they put into place was to establish regular family meetings. It was not easy. There was pushback from everyone. Emma initially resisted, feeling that the meetings were just another burden on top of her already stressful life. Liam was reluctant to share his feelings. Molly didn't know what to think. Even Lisa and Mark found it challenging to maintain a positive and open dialogue amidst their own busy schedules.

Despite the initial resistance, the family persevered. The meetings became a cornerstone for their progress and success, providing a safe space for each family member to express their feelings, share concerns, and discuss solutions.

CHAPTER 5 : EXTRAORDINARY LIVING

They began engaging in joint activities that brought joy and distraction from their challenges. One of the most transformative activities was gardening together.

The garden provided a beneficial outlet for the children's challenging behaviors. Emma's mood improved as she found a sense of control and accomplishment in planning and seeing the garden thrive. Liam's temper tantrums decreased as he channeled his energy into physical labor, which helped him release his frustrations. Molly's clinginess lessened as she found a sense of independence in the garden.

The Johnson family's success, despite their very real challenges, showcases the importance of not giving up, unity, and love within a family. Their story illustrates that mutual support and open communication can transform difficult times into opportunities for growth, connection, and extraordinary living!

Go where you are celebrated, not tolerated. If they can't see the real value of you, it's time for a new start.

— Unknown

Keyword for reflection: Releasing

› What or who are you holding onto that no longer serves you?
› What will it take for you to be able to truly release them?

We need to do a
better job of putting
ourselves higher on
our own "to-do" list.

— Michelle Obama

Keyword for reflection: Prioritize

› Do you know what your needs are?
› How can you take better care of them?

> For fast-acting relief,
> try slowing down.
>
> — Lily Tomlin

Keyword for reflection: Rest

› What can you do less of?
› When did you last rest without any distractions?
› What thoughts are you avoiding by keeping busy?

Do you realize that your love, your peace, your joy, your bliss can be so powerful in you that it becomes contagious, and people just want to be around you and they don't even know why.

— Lisa Nichols

Keyword for reflection: Attraction

› What do you focus on on a daily basis?
› How can you shift your focus toward abundance?
› What do you want more of in your life?
› Do you believe that what you focus on multiplies?

Chapter 6

Looking Back With Gratitude, Moving Forward With Hope

From being known simply as Teri to being lovingly referred to as Mom and from Mom to Dr. Teri, my journey has been nothing short of extraordinary. It's a story of resilience, self-empowerment, autonomous growth, and embracing opportunities to create a life filled with purpose and impact.

As a dedicated educator specializing in early intervention and behavior, I've found my passion in helping children and families unlock their potential and thrive. In my quest to nurture positive parenting, I developed the R*E*A*L* Peaceful Parenting framework for improving communication and more calmly resolving conflicts so peace can be restored in any home.

My journey also led me to become a reading and autism specialist, honing my skills to make a meaningful difference in the lives of those I work with. But my aspirations haven't stopped there.

Driven by a thirst for knowledge and a desire to share my expertise, I dived into the realm of educational coaching, empowering educators and parents alike to support and nurture young minds. My work takes me across the globe as an international speaker, sharing insights and strategies to create positive learning environments. I develop frameworks emphasizing differentiated instruction and cultural competence; conduct workshops to train educators on inclusive teaching practices; and organize seminars to empower parents with effective support strategies. I emphasize social-emotional learning, positive behavior support, and inclusive classroom design. The positive feedback from educators, parents, and students is immensely rewarding, confirming the impact of my work. Continuously learning and adapting to the evolving educational landscape, I remain committed to fostering environments where all students can do more than learn—they can flourish.

Writing is another avenue for me to reach and inspire a wider audience. I'm a celebrated author with multiple best-selling books that resonate not just nationally but internationally, touching hearts and minds with their messages.

I am also the proud creator of the Snuggle Bunny Book Club™, a reading haven for families to reconnect with each other and enjoy the wonders of literature and imagination.

Alongside these professional achievements, my greatest joy and accomplishment has been nurturing a loving, mutually respectful, and supportive relationship with my daughter. Parenthood taught me invaluable lessons in patience, empathy, and resilience, shaping me into the mother and woman I am today.

But life's tapestry isn't complete without the love and companionship of a partner who shares your dreams and aspirations. I am blessed to be happily married to Dr. Fred, a fellow entrepreneur and my partner in life. Together, we cherish moments of peace and tranquility on the shores of Rehoboth Bay, where our hearts find solace amidst nature's beauty. And, of course, GusGus, our beloved big brown dog, a furry companion, adds joy and laughter to our everyday adventures.

Reflecting on this journey, I am reminded that extraordinary lives are not built overnight. They are woven with resilience, empowerment, autonomy, and a relentless pursuit for growth. As Dr. Teri, educator, author, mentor, and mother, I continue to embrace each day as an opportunity to make a difference and inspire others to reach for their own extraordinary heights.

CHAPTER 6 : LOOKING BACK, MOVING FORWARD

A Life Well-Lived: Celebrating Your Achievements and Milestones

Now here is the BIG ask and the BIG promise ... to me and, more importantly, to yourself.

I want you to read and believe this quote by a silly old bear, and, after you sign this, *hang it up somewhere you can see it every single day!*

Promise me you'll always remember: You're braver than you believe, and stronger than you seem, and smarter than you think.

—A. A. Milne

Sign and date this as a reminder:

_____

A Note From Me To You

Dear Reader,

As I write this, I am filled with gratitude and hope. I am deeply honored to be included in your journey of self-discovery, empowerment, and transformation.

This book is not just a collection of quotes and stories; it is a testament to the strength and resilience that is within each of us. It is a reminder that no matter where we come from or what we have endured, we all have the power to create an extraordinary life. As you turn these pages, I hope that you will find the courage to face your challenges head-on, the inspiration to dream big, and the wisdom to trust in your own unique journey.

I, like you, have faced many obstacles and moments of doubt. I have known fear, loss, and the weight of uncertainty. But, in those moments, I discovered the incredible power of resilience, the strength that comes from within, and the beauty of living a life that is true to myself. And I know you can, too. You are not alone on this path. Your struggles, your dreams, your victories—they are all part of a shared human experience that connects us in profound and meaningful ways.

I encourage you to take these words to heart and let them be a guiding light on your journey. Reflect on the quotes, ponder the stories, and let your own experiences shape the lessons you take from them. Use this book as a tool to ignite your inner fire, to embrace your strengths, and to step boldly into the life you were meant to live.

Remember, the road to extraordinary living is not always easy, but it is always worth it. Each challenge you face is an opportunity to grow, each setback a chance to rise stronger, and each moment a precious gift.

May you find hope in times of despair, joy in moments of sadness, and the unwavering belief that you are capable of creating a life filled with purpose, passion, and unlimited possibilities.

Thank you for allowing me to be a part of your journey. I am cheering you on, and I believe in the extraordinary person that you are and the incredible life that you are destined to create.

With love and gratitude,

Dr. Teri Rouse

About the Author

Dr. Teri Rouse, Ed.D, or Dr. Teri to friends, family, students, and clients, has a mission to empower parents to overcome chaos and restore peace in their homes through a variety of techniques and strategies. Through her own life experiences, a love of learning, and a passion for helping families, she has dedicated her career to making a positive impact on children, parents, and educators.

Working with students and private clients from diverse cultural and socioeconomic backgrounds, she develops and implements customized positive behavior interventions. Taking the best of the best strategies and techniques, she created the R*E*A*L* Peaceful Parenting framework. She also has a program for young adults called Braver Than You Believe to guide them to overcome fear and worry, gain confidence, and discover their inner strength.

Dr. Teri has spent more than thirty years in classrooms as a special education teacher, behavior and early interventionist, autism specialist, and applied behavior analyst, in addition to founding and serving as the managing director of KIDS: Interventions & Direct Services. Additionally, for seventeen years, Dr. Teri has taught teachers how to teach at Chestnut Hill College, Widener University, and Penn State.

An educational coach and consultant and international speaker, she travels the globe to give presentations at conferences for teachers, school administrators, organizations, and conventions. She is involved with the Division of International Special Education and Services, the Council for Exceptional Children (CEC), Autism Speaks, Lily's Hope Foundation, and Uthando, a South African nonprofit tourism and community development initiative.

Dr. Teri has authored multiple bestselling books, including *Untamed Chaos*, and is a member of the National Academy of Best-Selling Authors® and a recipient of the Quilly® Award for *Success* with Jack Canfield and *Never*

Give Up with Dick Vitale. Inspired by decades of working with children, she authored *Julian's Gift*, a picture book that tells the story of one young boy in her class. In addition, Dr. Teri created the Snuggle Bunny Book Club™, a subscription service that enables families to bond over hand-picked, engaging books delivered weekly.

She has been featured on ABC, CBS, NBC, FOX News, Bravo, the Success Network, *USA Today*, *Miami Herald*, Boston.com, and more.

For more information about Dr. Teri and her programs, visit:

drterirouse.com
Facebook: Dr. Teri Rouse
Instagram: dr_teri_rouse

www.ingramcontent.com/pod-product-compliance
Lightning Source LLC
Chambersburg PA
CBHW062022050526
44107CB00106B/968